WILDFLOWERS
across TEXAS

WILDFLOWERS across TEXAS

Photography by
LAURENCE PARENT

Foreword by
LAURA BUSH

Essay by
PATRICIA CAPERTON PARENT

Graphic Arts Center Publishing®

To our parents,
Annette and Hiram Parent,
and Patsie and James Caperton

An imprint of Graphic Arts Center Publishing Company
P.O. Box 10306, Portland, Oregon 97296-0306
503-266-2402; www.gacpc.com

ACKNOWLEDGMENTS

We wish to thank botanists Tom Wendt, B. L. Turner, Andrew McDonald, and Bonnie Crozier of the University of Texas at Austin Plant Resources Center for help with identifying flowers. Special thanks go also to Laura Bush and Mary Margaret Farabee, and to Al Summerfield and Judith Guthrie of Summerfield's Wagons for their indispensable help with this book.

Library of Congress Cataloging-in-Publication Data:

   Parent, Laurence.

     Wildflowers across Texas / foreword by Laura Bush ;

    essay by Patricia Caperton Parent ;

    photos by Laurence Parent.

      p. cm.

    ISBN 1-55868-643-6 (hardbound)

     1. Photography of plants—Texas. 2. Wild flowers—Texas—Pictorial works.

   I. Parent, Patricia Caperton. II. Title.

   TR724 .P37 2002

   582.13'09764—dc21

2001008038

President: Charles M. Hopkins
Associate Publisher: Douglas A. Pfeiffer
Editorial Staff: Timothy W. Frew, Ellen Harkins Wheat, Tricia Brown,
   Kathy Matthews, Jean Bond-Slaughter
Production Staff: Richard L. Owsiany,
   Joanna M. Goebel
Cover Design: Elizabeth Watson
Interior Design: Jean Andrews
Printer: Haagen Printing
Bindery: Lincoln *&* Allen Co.

Printed in the United States of America

◁ ◁ *Native iris* (Iris hexagona),
Palmetto State Park.
◁ *Bluebonnets* (Lupinus texensis),
Inks Lake State Park, Hill Country.
▷ *Morning glories* (Ipomoea leptophylla),
Alibates Flint Quarries
National Monument.

FOREWORD

by Laura Bush

As a wise person once said, "In every walk with nature, one receives far more than he seeks." This statement rings especially true in Texas when the wildflowers are in full bloom.

From the piney woods of East Texas to the desert oasis of El Paso, from the shores of the Gulf Coast to the plains of the Panhandle, wildflowers can be found in every region of the Lone Star State almost year-round. Those who stroll among them and soak up their beauty come away feeling richly rewarded.

Fanciful wildflower stories are passed down from generation to generation. Bluebonnets are bits of the sky that have drifted down and settled over the ground like bright blue blankets. Buttercups spring up where the sun has kissed the earth. If a child holds the tiny yellow flower under her chin and her skin glows yellow, she is said to like butter. A colorful flower is the prickly pear cactus's annual peace offering for its usually thorny company.

We owe Mother Nature a great deal for the delicate miracles that somehow survive—even thrive—both on and off the beaten path. Before Texas had boundaries, the state had wildflowers, but truth be told, Lady Bird Johnson sowed the seeds for the explosion of roadside color that blossoms every spring. Americans cannot mention one without praising the other.

Wildflowers are seasonal historians that offer unbiased accounts of climate and weather. In times of drought, sparse, faded flowers with parched tongues speak of hot sun and dry soil. When the wind is cooler and the dry climate is tempered by rain, traces give way to bright patches of color. Healthy green stalks produce plump flowers that sing the joys of well-nourished roots, and onlookers sense the drought is broken—for a while, anyway.

Every year the state's wildflowers delight and inspire—especially in the Central Texas spring, when people come out in droves to take pictures among the bluebonnets blooming in fields and along roads. Journey from Central Texas down to the Gulf Coast, and you'll find carpets of red flowers known as Indian blankets.

◁ *Big Bend bluebonnets* (Lupinus havardii) *and ribbon of margined perityle* (Perityle vaseyi) *near Castolon, Big Bend National Park.*

7

△ *Rock nettle* (Eucnide bartonioides),
Big Bend Ranch State Park.

▷ *Indian blankets* (Gaillardia pulchella),
Cleburne State Park.

Travel to East Texas, and the blankets of blue give way to rich hues of yellow, orange, and red. There you might find the cardinal flower nestled among flowering azaleas near a cool, shallow stream.

In West Texas, the agave takes so long to bloom that it was given the nickname "century plant." Its towering flowers stand smartly against any desert backdrop.

From North-Central Texas to the Panhandle you'll see little brown, red, and yellow flowers bobbing in hot, late-summer breezes. These bear a striking resemblance to sombreros and are fondly referred to as "Mexican hats."

Flower lovers go to great lengths to preserve wildflowers. You'll find the little treasures pressed between the pages of Bibles, immortalized in family photographs, penciled on the pages of history books, and captured in museum-quality paintings sealed behind climate-controlled glass.

No need to visit a gallery or the great outdoors to steal a glance at Texas's legendary wildflowers, though. Just turn the pages of this beautiful book. Within its covers you'll find a visual feast that rivals the real thing. Laurence Parent has done a marvelous job of capturing both Texas wildflowers and our imagination in this carefully prepared and richly finished book.

I hope you enjoy this colorful journey across Lone Star soil as much as this native Texan does. I may be partial to its contents, but I predict this is a book you'll want to visit again and again.

◁ *Dogwood tree* (Cornus florida), *Wild Azalea Canyon, Newton County.*

△ *Cenizo* (Leucophyllum frutescens) *and yucca, Black Gap Wildlife Management Area, Dead Horse Mountains.*

▷ ▷ *Bluebonnets* (Lupinus subcarnosus), *Texas groundsel* (Senecio ampullaceus), *and a white prickly poppy*
(Argemone albiflora) *at Summerfield's Wagons, Gonzales County.*

△ *Mexican hats* (Ratibida columnifera), *Enchanted Rock State Natural Area.*
▷ *Giant dagger yucca* (Yucca faxoniana), *Dead Horse Mountains, Big Bend National Park.*

TEXAS WILDFLOWERS

by Patricia Caperton Parent

Where flowers bloom, so does hope.
—Lady Bird Johnson

Native Texans, with legendary pride, say everything's bigger and better in Texas. While that may or may not be true, Texas is a land of striking contrasts and vast distances, a place of rugged mountains, sandy seashores, shady pine forests, live oak-covered hills, broad meadows, and tabletop-flat plains that stretch forever toward the horizon. Texans love their state, embracing it, making it part of them, firmly believing it's the best possible place to be. They love their wildflowers, too.

Texas wildflowers adorn and complement this land, accentuating its contrasts. Most people think of wildflowers as low-growing plants blanketing sunny fields and meadows, but wildflowers grow on vines, bushes, cacti, and even tall trees. Some wildflowers throw themselves at you, while others hide in shady spots and nestle beneath other plants. Who can miss a deep blue field of bluebonnets peppered with purplish red phlox and colorful Indian paintbrush? Yet a lone, delicate columbine hidden near a running stream takes more effort to discover. Some wildflowers thrive in water; others flourish in the desert. At Brazos Bend State Park, along the Gulf Coast, lily pads in oxbow lakes boast cheerful white flowers, while out west in Big Bend National Park, huge dagger yuccas dot the desert floor and mountain slopes, their blooms reaching boldly toward the desert sky. Goat-foot morning glories hug shifting dunes near the warm Gulf of Mexico, while Mexican catch-flies grace cool, shady areas high in the Guadalupe Mountains. Many Texas wildflowers create a show with a single, spectacular bloom, but others crowd next to one another, forming striking carpets of undulating color. Some wildflowers hug the ground, while others, such as those of the Texas redbud tree, create early spring swatches of purple against still-dormant forest canopies.

◁ *Milk vetch* (Astragalus giganteus), *Davis Mountains.*

❧❧❧

Wildflowers nourish the human spirit. They surprise our eyes with color and enchant us with exhilarating fragrances. A vibrant field of wildflowers soothes the soul, reassuring us of hope, reminding us of new horizons. The flowers' very fragility reaffirms life and links us to nature. Because their colors and fragrances exist only briefly, we lament their passing but rest assured that we'll see them again next year.

Both ephemeral and eternal, wildflowers intimately connect us with the circle of life. While they may seem merely ornamental, they are, as are all flowers, essential to plants' survival. Since plants provide oxygen, shelter, and food for other life, their reproduction is crucial to human survival. Most plants reproduce through pollination, the transfer of pollen grains from the male anther to the female stigma in a plant's flowers. This can occur within the same flower or between flowers, depending on the species. Flowers can have male, female, or sometimes both structures.

Ninety percent of flowering plants need animals to pollinate them, and their flowers exist for one reason—to attract pollinators. The color patterns, shapes, scents, nectar, pollen, and even blooming times of flowers are all designed to lure specific animals. Animals depend on flowers, in turn, for food and, in some cases, reproduction, further strengthening the bonds between all living things.

Most people just enjoy flowers, giving little thought to why blossoms may be shaped or colored in a particular way. Yet color, shape, and pattern reveal much about a flower's relationship with its pollinator. Flowers must compete with one another to attract insects and birds, and over time specific flowers have evolved to attract specific pollinators. Color is one defining aspect. Different pollinators see different color ranges. Butterflies, birds, and flies respond to red and yellow colors, as you know if you've ever seen a hungry hummingbird hone in on a bright red feeder. Bees, one of the most important pollinators, see toward the blue end of the human visible spectrum, even to the near-ultraviolet. They don't see red, but will visit red flowers, perhaps attracted by ultraviolet patterns invisible to the human eye. Nocturnal moths and bats find large white or very pale-colored flowers most easily. The distinctive bull's-eye patterns of coreopsis, sunflowers, and coneflowers provide a stark contrast to green foliage, creating a recognizable pattern even if the pollinator cannot see the entire color range.

△ *Purple coneflowers* (Echinacea *sp.*) *Lake Texoma, Eisenhower State Park.*

Wildflowers come in an infinite variety of shapes, designed not to please us—although that's a delightful bonus—but to make pollination easy and effective. Animals often depend on flower pollen or nectar for food, and flowers have evolved to accommodate the most efficient pollinators. Because butterflies need a place to perch while drinking nectar, they prefer wide flowers with firm petals. Moths hover when feeding, so strong petals aren't important to them; flowers dependent on moths often hang downward to assure contact. Flowers with deep nectaries attract bees, whose long tongues let them get at nectar that other insects can't. Tube-shaped flowers, with their reservoirs of nectar, sustain hummingbirds, whose rapid metabolism requires constant nourishment. Many insects spread pollen around as they eat it. Beetles have big appetites and need flowers, such as poppies, that grow close together and generate lots of easily accessible pollen. These large insects lurch from flower to flower, collecting and sprinkling pollen as they go. Pitcher plants, with their elegant curves, attract pollinating insects only to trap and digest them in a pool of fluid.

Even the sweet flower scents that remind us of spring and summer and stir our memories are designed as bait for pollinators. Many animals have a much keener sense of smell than humans and can easily differentiate among flower species. Many flowers, once pollinated, abruptly change scents, signaling the pollinator to move elsewhere.

Luckily for us, the variety of colors, shapes, and fragrances of wildflowers creates a feast for the soul and the senses. In Texas, the feast is nearly year-round.

❧❧❧

△ *Bluebonnets* (Lupinus texensis), *Indian paintbrush* (Castilleja indivisa), *and verbena* (Glandularia bipinnatifida *var.* bipinnatifida), *Hays County.*

Texans have always had a special relationship with their wildflowers. Declared the official state flower in 1901, the bluebonnet symbolizes Texas as much as the longhorn, cowboy, oil well, or ten-gallon hat. This cone-shaped, purplish blue wildflower features delicate flowerets stacked intricately on a long stem, crowned by light blue to white flowerets at the top. If you use a little imagination, the flowerets resemble faces underneath bonnets. Bluebonnets grow across much of the state but flourish in Central Texas and can be seen on caps, postcards, T-shirts—almost any souvenir representing Texas. In an annual spring pilgrimage, Texans flock to the countryside to view the blue blooms and revel in their sweet, grapelike fragrance. It's not unusual to see carloads of camera-toting tourists parked along roadsides, positioning one another for the best shot among the flowers. No Texas family photo album is complete without an image of freshly scrubbed kids surrounded by bluebonnets and decked out in their Sunday best.

Just as bluebonnets are synonymous with Texas, Lady Bird Johnson—former First Lady and widow of President Lyndon B. Johnson—is synonymous with wildflowers. In the 1960s, inspired by Texas wildflowers, Mrs. Johnson began a national public-awareness campaign to educate Americans about preserving natural beauty. Her efforts eventually resulted in Congress passing the Highway Beautification Act of 1965, which encourages improved roadside landscaping. Back home in Texas, Mrs. Johnson continued to work tirelessly to preserve and promote Texas wildflowers. In 1982, in an effort to inspire others through education, she founded the nonprofit National Wildflower Research Center, known today as the Lady Bird Johnson Wildflower Center.

The Wildflower Center, a beautifully designed facility located in Austin, draws visitors from all corners of the state and much of the nation. Here, the public can learn about the many ecological benefits of native plants. The Center features Texas flora in cultivated gardens and undeveloped fields alike, along with plenty of educational information for anyone wanting to learn more about wildflowers. A rainwater collection and storage system provides sustenance without depleting the underground aquifer. Classrooms and auditoriums accommodate seminars and conferences. Best of all, on a warm spring day, a stroll through the Center's gardens and hiking trails reveals a treasure trove of Texas blooms.

Texans take their wildflowers seriously. Each year, the Texas Department of Transportation seeds highway rights-of-way with forty-seven thousand pounds of wildflower seed. Each pound contains thirty varieties. Although many states seed wildflowers today, Texas has been doing it for more than six decades, longer than any other. During peak season, the Department of Transportation maintains a wildflower hotline describing the best viewing spots and mows only after the flowers have gone to seed.

Past generations of Texans usually got in their cars and traveled to see wildflowers—and many still do—but lots of present-day Texans are enjoying wildflowers at home, too. Growing native wildflowers is easy and fun. Xeriscaping, a low-maintenance, low-water-use form of landscaping, is rising in popularity. Years of successive droughts in many parts of Texas have taxed common water resources, forcing homeowners to rethink landscape design. A plethora of xeriscape and native-plant gardening books and websites serve the growing need to turn back to these hardy native species. More and more Texas yards include beds of cheerful wildflowers. In some cases, homeowners have removed their water-hungry grass and turned traditional front lawns into wildflower-studded grounds.

Of course, picking or digging up existing wildflowers isn't the recommended or legal way to start a native wildflower garden. Commercially grown wildflower seeds are widely available. Fittingly, the nation's largest working wildflower seed farm, Wildseed Farms, is located in Central Texas near Fredricksburg. Wildseed cultivates wildflowers on fifteen hundred acres and harvests the seeds for commercial sale, creating brilliantly hued fields in the process. Because each plot supports an individual species, the color is usually monochromatic, unlike the fitful, random splatters nature offers. Travelers along Highway 290, accustomed to landscapes of gently rolling Hill Country pastures dotted with live oak and grazing cattle, can't help abruptly slowing down at the sight of neatly squared-off acres of bright red, yellow, or blue rippling in the sun. The farm has become a tourist attraction in its own right, attracting thousands of visitors each year.

Across Texas Seasons

Many wildflowers follow a seasonal pattern linked to cyclical changes in sunlight, temperature, and rainfall, although desert wildflowers are often opportunistic, blooming on the heels of random rainfall. Variations in latitude, altitude, and precipitation patterns mean that some of the same species may bloom at different times and in more or less profusion, but nevertheless they roughly follow nature's clock. Most Texas wildflowers bloom in spring, which comes earlier to Texas than to much of the nation. Wildflower blooms begin in late January to early February in the southern and low-altitude parts of the state and then spread northward and up into the higher elevations, usually reaching their peak in April.

Throughout Texas, the rate of new blooms slows down by May, but it doesn't stop. By June, few new wildflowers are blooming except in North Texas and the Panhandle, and the rate of new blooms has slowed down here as well, yielding to the hot Texas summers.

Early to mid-July is hot and dry. Too late for spring rains and too early for late-summer monsoons, July presents a survival challenge to flowering and nonflowering plants alike. Relief may come in the form of an early tropical storm

▷ *Nonnative crimson clover* (Trifolium incarnatum) *and coreopsis* (Coreopsis grandiflora), *Houston County.*

20

off the Gulf, but this is rare. If such a storm does blow in, or spotty thunderstorms create sporadic rains, opportunistic summer wildflowers such as mealy blue sage may produce blooms. Overall, though, this is a time of fading wildflowers and increasing heat.

Hot, dry weather continues in late July and August throughout most of the state, except far West Texas, where late summer brings monsoonal afternoon thunderstorms to the arid terrain. Mornings start sunny, but by afternoon, thunderheads darken the sky and release welcome, cooling rain in brief, often heavy downpours. Dry, hot, and brown since May, the land rapidly turns a lush green. Higher elevations in the Texas mountains receive even more moisture than the basins below. Renewed and replenished, opportunistic flowers bloom from alpine meadows to desert basins, including shrubby scarlet bouvardia, yellow milk vetch, desert poppies, dayflowers, and yellow trumpet flowers.

Throughout Texas, September brings more rain than summer does as tropical weather rolls in from the Gulf of Mexico and a few weak cold fronts blow south across the plains. A few hardy wildflowers begin their blooms in this month. Asters particularly like September. Small, white heath asters flourish all over Texas. Still, most of the state's September wildflowers aren't as striking as their spring cousins. Numerous small, white or muted yellow flowers growing together in clumps replace the large, bright, colorful flowers of spring. The ubiquitous goldenrod typifies Texas fall flowers. It features tiny, unimpressive dull gold flowers, but when bunched together, they create broad swaths of gold across the landscape.

By October, cold fronts have become more frequent, and by late in the month a rare early snow may dust the Panhandle. Few wildflowers begin blooming, save for the prickly, nonnative sow thistle. In Central and West Texas, the golden-eye offers attractive yellow blooms.

November offers much of the same, with much cooler temperatures. Throughout Texas, the ruffled fringed puccoon unfolds bright yellow flowers in sandy soils and woody uplands.

Just because most Texas wildflowers don't offer their first blooms in fall doesn't mean the landscape is barren. The common dandelion, rock rose, and Dakota vervain bloom all year with optimal circumstances. A warm, rainy fall without a freeze can keep some wildflowers blooming right into early winter. I've seen healthy Indian blankets blooming on Galveston Island in late November.

But a period of dormancy, devoid of color and razzle-dazzle, isn't all bad. It's the launching pad for spring renewal. Many Texas wildflowers begin growth during fall, remain quiescent through winter's cold, and then explode in a riot of color with spring's arrival. Next time you look at bare trees and brown, frostbitten grass, think about the palette of color awaiting longer, warmer days.

Across the Texas Landscape

As the second-largest state in the nation, Texas encompasses a much greater diversity of landscapes than most other states. It serves as a meeting place of vastly different geographical regions, each with a unique combination of climates, soils, and terrains. The deserts and mountains of far West Texas look very unlike the piney woods of East Texas, and the Panhandle has an entirely different climate than that of the Gulf Coast.

△ *Bluebonnets* (Lupinus subcarnosus) *and phlox* (Phlox cuspidata), *Bastrop County.*

Classifying regions is difficult, though, with as many opinions about how to describe Texas geography as there are Texans. Yet it's important to do, because a region's temperature, precipitation, altitude, and soil have an enormous effect on what kinds of wildflowers live there and where and when they grow and bloom. It's also interesting to know that, in Texas, longitude creates more variance in climate than latitude, as rainfall rates decrease greatly from east to west. With all this in mind when discussing Texas wildflowers, we can divide the state into six broad regions: East Texas, the Gulf Coast, Central Texas, North Texas, the Panhandle, and West Texas.

East Texas

East Texas makes up roughly the eastern fourth of the state. Most of the land is low and flat, with gently rolling hills in the northern part. This northern section receives a bit less rain than the southern part, but all over East Texas, lush forests and grassy prairies abound. Bald cypress trees thrive along bayous, creeks, lakes, and in swampy areas. High humidity, about fifty inches of rain a year, and a temperate climate provide a long and productive growing season. With its morning fog and Spanish moss-covered trees, this area looks and feels like part of the Old South. Forests of pine, beech, magnolia, oak, sweetgum, and black hickory blanket acidic, sandy soil. The Big Thicket area is known as one of the most complex forest systems in the United States, containing nearly a thousand flowering plants.

Wildflowers can begin blooming in the southern part of East Texas by late January, but peak in March and April. White patches of spring beauties and blue violet patches of small bluets can show up in January and are almost inevitable by February. In March, white dogwood trees burst into bloom, their popcorn-like white blossoms standing out against the deep green pines, spring leaf buds, and still-dormant trees. Beneath the trees, wild azaleas welcome spring with showy, pinkish white blooms.

A very interesting wildflower also starts its bloom in East Texas in March. In damp, boggy areas of Southeast Texas, insect-eating pitcher plants sport their greenish yellow, upside-down flowers. The plant's main stalk resembles a skinny vase with a wide, partially covered top. Drawn by the scent, hungry, unwary insects seek the pitcher plant's nectar, but when they touch the flower, they slide down its slick hairs into the fluid-filled bottom, where the plant's digestive juices devour them. If you hike in marshy, open areas of the Big Thicket in early spring, you're sure to find patches of these carnivorous wildflowers. Whenever I encounter them, I kneel down, take a closer look, and marvel at such an ingenious adaptation.

△ *Winecups* (Callirhoe *sp.*) *and wild onion* (Allium *sp.*), *Hays County.*

The refined, snowy white spider lily thrives throughout East Texas from March through May, growing along stream banks and ditches and in meadows in regularly flooded areas. Spider lily flowers can grow to seven inches across and have long, narrow petals resembling their namesake's legs. The fragrant white flowers contrast sharply with the dark, brackish water often found near them.

△ *Magnolia blossom*
(Magnolia grandiflora),
Brazoria County.

East Texas wildflowers aren't always typical—you may have to look up rather than down to see them. Southern magnolia trees, which can grow to ninety feet tall, display one of the largest and most beautiful flowers in the state. Even if you can't reach them, you can easily spot these big, ivory-colored flowers against the magnolia's broad, dark green leaves. The sweet-smelling blossom lasts only about two to three days, but during early summer a mature magnolia will create many new ones with every sunrise. When I was growing up, we had a young Southern magnolia tree in our front yard. During bloom season I would climb up into its branches, sometimes venturing precariously out along shaky limbs in search of blossoms to pick so my mom could put them in a vase. Since the flowers are about the size of a dinner plate, they weren't particularly easy to pick, required a very large vase, and quickly turned from milky white to brown no matter what we did—but they were luscious while they lasted.

The Gulf Coast

The Gulf Coast stretches along the Gulf of Mexico and a few miles inland from Texas's border with Louisiana to its border with Mexico. From one end to the other, the land is flat and sandy, with hardly any rocks. Along much of the coast, long, narrow barrier islands parallel the shore, stretching protectively in front of shallow bays and estuaries. Few trees grow on the islands or near the beach; instead, salt grass and salt marshes flourish just beyond the dune line. In the eastern half of the Gulf Coast region, where rainfall averages about forty-four inches a year, large water oaks and other coastal trees thrive a few miles inland. In the much drier western half, scrubby chaparral of cactus, mesquite, dwarf oak, and huisache dot the inland terrain.

Here, the Gulf of Mexico governs life. Its warm waters temper winter's cold; winter freezes occur infrequently. The Gulf's sea breezes send moisture inland, where it clashes with cooler air to create much-needed rain. Usually the Gulf is placid, but in late summer and early fall, tropical storms and fierce hurricanes occasionally come from the south, drawing on the warm tropical water for strength. As these storms build, they create strong winds and huge waves and generate copious amounts of rain. If the storms move northward and slam into Texas with all their fury, they can rearrange the flat coastline, barrier islands, dunes, and even waterways. Sometimes hurricanes spin far into Texas, spawning flash floods as they go.

Despite the salty air, shifting sands, and sometimes raging tides, salt-tolerant wildflowers survive and even flourish here. Warm winters and humid summers allow wildflowers to begin blooming as early as January. Field pansies can decorate inland fields, pastures, and woodland meadows even before the grass turns green. Gulf Coast wildflowers peak in March and April. Along the southwest coast, white dandelions offer their cheerful March blossoms, while yellow camphor daisies begin blooming in the central coast area. All along the Texas coast, colonies of pale blue Texas toadflax wave their spiky flowers in the Gulf breeze. Many Gulf Coast wildflowers bloom throughout the summer and often continue blooming into early winter.

Although many people don't associate the Gulf Coast with wildflowers, if you look carefully, you can find incredible pockets of beauty. Coastal wild-flowers aren't as flashy or as prolific as some in other regions, but they're worth looking for. An early morning walk along the beach can reveal a delicate strand of bright pink goat foot morning glories hugging a dune ridge, following its windswept curves with perfect symmetry. Among the sea oats and cordgrass, patches of yellow dune primrose provide a bright contrast to the sea and sky. In summer, sea ox-eyes and common sunflowers add to the yellow palette. These flowers are useful as well as beautiful. Creeping plants such as morning glories send out long runners that help secure loose, shifting sand, and upright plants' far-reaching roots bind sand, slowing wind erosion and preserving dunes.

In flat areas inland from the dunes, other wildflowers flourish. In fall, waves of orange-colored goldenrod (often confused with ragweed) sway in the sea breeze. Prickly pear cacti thrive here, too, displaying their flamboyant flowers whenever a rainy period gives them the chance.

Central Texas

Most wildflower aficionados think of Central Texas when they picture Texas wild-flowers. Many of the state's best-known wildflowers bloom here in profusion, including bluebonnets, Indian paintbrush, and Drummond phlox. Located, clearly, in the center of the state, Central Texas features hilly terrain ranging from gently rolling in the east to quite rugged in the west, especially on the Edwards Plateau. The Plateau is located north and west of the Balcones Fault line, an abrupt escarpment running east from Del Rio to San Antonio and northeast from San Antonio toward Waco. On the Edwards Plateau, thin alkaline soils predominate, loosely covering a thick bed of limestone. Clear, spring-fed rivers such as the Comal and San Marcos gush out of the hills from natural springs, and seasonal creeks cut rugged canyons through rocky limestone hills. Large cattle, sheep, and goat ranches abound, but many are being subdivided as the region's cities grow. Live oaks, cedar elms, and hardy junipers thrive just about everywhere. Around Llano, the limestone yields to granite, but the flora changes little. In places, round pink-granite domes push up toward the sky, buttons against a sea of pastel green foliage. Texans call this part of Central Texas the Hill Country.

East and south of the Edwards Plateau, toward Bryan-College Station, soils are richer and the terrain is flatter and much less rocky. Lusher vegetation means that smaller farms replace the Hill Country's sprawling ranches. Fewer trees dot the landscape, and wide-open fields provide ideal wild-flower habitat.

Central Texas's climate is cooler than the Gulf Coast's. Freezes are common, but extremely low winter temperatures are not. Summers are hot, with an average July high of ninety-five degrees. Rainfall averages about twenty-eight inches a year, although it's slightly wetter in the east and slightly drier in the west. Spring is the wettest time. If spring rains don't come, wildflowers often don't show up in force either; but if nature's timing is just right, expect an extravagant show as wildflowers begin blooming in late February and peak in April.

Lots of wildflowers flourish throughout Central Texas. In a good spring, bluebonnets blanket hill after hill like an upside-down blue sky. As legumes, bluebonnets return much-needed nitrogen to the soil, making it more fertile. Purplish red Drummond phlox, bright red Indian paintbrush, and yellow

△ *Bluebonnets* (Lupinus texensis) *and Indian paintbrush* (Castilleja indivisa), *Llano County, Hill Country.*

bladderpod sometimes swirl among the blue like Technicolor clouds. When these flowers bloom sans bluebonnets, they cut swaths of lustrous color across spring green fields. Here and there, ubiquitous prickly pear cacti peek up above the traditional ground-hugging wildflower species, breaking out in yellow bouquets.

Bluebonnets, phlox, and paintbrush are enough to take one's breath away, but these impressive specimens are by no means the only wildflowers gracing Central Texas fields and hills. Low-growing prairie verbena, with its small flowers and dark purple hues, provides a pleasing background for taller, flashier flowers. Yellow huisache daisies, purple baby blue-eyes, and delicate, white, wild onion flowers also furnish subtle backdrops of color for Central Texas's wildflower "stars."

Other spring Central Texas wildflowers include the flamboyant white prickly poppy, which features a large, crinkled flower. Plains fleabane, bull nettle, and trout lilies add more variety. On warm, sunny mornings, dwarf dandelions open their small flowers, yielding a brief splash of yellow. Purple spiderworts grace the morning meadows, closing their delicate flowers when the afternoon sun becomes too intense.

Many Texans travel to Central Texas for the region's spring bloom. On weekends, numerous wildflower seekers cruise the back roads, searching for that perfect flower patch. When I was a college student in San Marcos, my friends and I would crowd into a car and drive around the nearby Hill Country looking for blooms. Once, we found a thick patch of bluebonnets along the road and stopped to take pictures. As we were getting into place, another car full of students stopped and got out, ooohing and aaahing over the grape-scented flowers. We didn't know them, but soon we all were posing together in the flowers like old friends, arms around one another. Although they're a little dog-eared, I still have those photos today, a cheerful reminder of youth and a long-ago Central Texas spring.

Not all Central Texas wildflowers grow along roadsides and in fields. Spring visitors to swampy Palmetto State Park delight in the ornately shaped wild irises blooming in its marshes. And no spring would be complete without the grape-Kool-Aid–scented clusters of purple flowers hanging from the scrappy but beautiful mountain laurel.

North Texas

North Texas comprises approximately the upper fourth of the state, excluding the Panhandle, from Abilene eastward. Here, north-south strips of cross timbers—scrubby woodlands of post oaks, cedar elms, hackberries, and hickories growing in thick, sandy soil—alternate with north-south strips of rolling prairies. The climate is much like Central Texas's, although winters are colder. Rainfall averages about thirty-three inches a year, with rates declining from east to west. Vegetation flourishes in the eastern part, while the westernmost area is almost desolate, with far fewer trees. Fierce ice storms occasionally blanket North Texas in winter, making travel treacherous and breaking tree limbs and power lines. Major rivers, including the Trinity and the Brazos, flow lazily through this country. The Red River, so named because of the colorful sand it collects on its journey, forms Texas's northern boundary with Oklahoma. North Texas land is mostly flat to lightly rolling, with mesas appearing in the drier west. In the cross-timbers area, the soil is thin and sandy, but in the eastern part of the region, the Blackland Prairie represents some of the most fertile land in the state. Before settlement, the sod was thick and fertile, nourishing lush, tall prairie grasses and numerous wildflowers.

Today, most of the land in the eastern part is cultivated farmland; very little of the original prairie remains. Nonetheless, several wildflower species bloom abundantly here. Bloom season starts and peaks a bit later than in Central Texas. Many of the same wildflowers that bloomed earlier farther south start and peak in North Texas in May and June. Indian blankets and horsemint carpet the prairies with deep color in May. Plains wallflowers and lemon paintbrush add dashes of yellow. If cool nights and temperate days prevail, many of these flowers will bloom through June and often into July.

Purple coneflowers flourish throughout North Texas but grow especially well along the rocky shores of Lake Texoma, one of the largest lakes in Texas. These distinctive pinkish flowers, with long, leafless stems and narrow petals turned down in an almost sad fashion, begin blooming in May and can continue

△ *Carolina jessamine* (Gelsemium sempervirens), *Newton County.*

well into summer. If you take a late-spring walk along the bluffs above Lake Texoma in Eisenhower State Park, you can't miss the scores of purple coneflowers perched along the edge.

In June, newly blooming wildflowers include foxglove, Texas thistle, and purple prairie clover. Perky bluebells (beautiful, upright, deeply cupped blue purple flowers that look nothing like bluebonnets) decorate the area throughout the hot summer. Wine-cups, colored just like red wine and shaped much like a wine glass, profusely pepper North Texas meadows with flecks of effervescent color. Pink showy primroses or yellow Missouri primroses, sometimes better known as buttercups, can cover North Texas fields like a brightly hued blanket. If either primrose variety's sweet scent tempts you to stick your nose into the flower, you're likely to get a dusting of yellow pollen. When I was a little girl, I used to love to smell the buttercups until the tip of my nose turned yellow with pollen.

The Panhandle

The Panhandle—the part of Texas that protrudes up into the Great Plains—features some of the flattest landscape in the United States. Land and sky seem to stretch forever, merging together on a distant, unbroken horizon. The wind blows hard and fast and just about all the time. It cools summer nights but also ushers in fast-moving blue northers in winter, sometimes dropping the temperature fifty degrees in half an hour. Panhandle winters are real winters, complete with ice and snow and even occasional blizzards. The climate is drier here than in much of the rest of the state, with annual rainfall averaging about sixteen inches. The unremitting wind endlessly frustrates wildflower photographers, who need their subjects to be motionless for at least a few seconds.

Because much of the flattest part of the Panhandle is cultivated for cotton, corn, sorghum, and peanuts, few wildflowers can complete their life cycles without being disturbed. Even if you look hard, you won't find many wildflowers in cultivated areas. Just east of Lubbock, however, the High Plains drop abruptly into the lower Rolling Plains, forming a dramatic geological feature called the Caprock Escarpment. Along the Caprock, deep canyons cut through red sandstone. Sculpted by the wind and rain, bizarre twisted rock formations reach toward the sky. Trees, grasses, and, yes, wildflowers flourish among the crumbling sandstone and trickling creeks.

Spring wildflowers bloom late in the Panhandle because it's farther north than the rest of Texas. In June, Indian blankets—red, disk-shaped flowers with a narrow yellow ring around the outside of the petals—dot the ground like tossed coins. Here and there among the Indian blankets, spiky-shaped purple horsemint flowers stick up over the sea of red and yellow. Basket flowers add touches of lavender to the mix.

One June afternoon at Caprock Canyons State Park, I walked along the edge of a canyon that was literally surrounded by acres of Indian blankets in peak bloom. They grew tightly together along the canyon rim and spilled down the canyon walls. Looking across the canyon, I could see copper-red patch after copper-red patch on the other side. Occasionally a thick stand of purple horsemint broke the pattern, its tall blooms wafting their delightful lemony scent to

me along the perpetual Panhandle wind. On the horizon, building cumulo-nimbus clouds signaled an approaching thunderstorm. As the dark clouds grew closer, the light became softer, and the reds, yellows, and purples turned almost luminous. I knew I should hustle back to our campsite, but I lingered, awed by the kaleidoscope of color before me.

∧ *Giant dagger yuccas* (Yucca faxoniana), *Dagger Flat, Big Bend National Park.*

West Texas

West Texas is big country, with all the features of a classic Southwest landscape. It has tall mountains, flat-topped mesas, pine forests, alpine meadows, cool streams, baking deserts, lots of cacti, and spectacular, breathtaking views. It stretches roughly from west of San Angelo to El Paso, including the Rio Grande's Big Bend and excluding the Panhandle. The far western part, known as the Trans Pecos, contains Texas's thirty-plus named mountain ranges, including the well-known Guadalupe, Chisos, Davis, and Franklin Ranges. Most have peaks more than a mile high and tend to be cooler and wetter than the surrounding desert.

Rainfall, or the lack of it, affects every living thing here, including wild-flowers. Most of the region receives less than twelve inches of rain a year, although some of the higher elevations get more. Due to sporadic precipitation, many West Texas wildflowers are more opportunistic than seasonal, although many prefer spring.

29

Winters can be cold, with occasional snow, but West Texas warms up fast in spring, particularly the Big Bend area. Several wildflowers begin blooming and peak in late February and March, including Torrey yuccas and the evening-blooming datura. If fall and winter rains have been better than average, by late February Big Bend National Park is awash in Big Bend bluebonnets, sometimes known as Chisos bluebonnets. Nearly three feet tall, Big Bend bluebonnets are truly Texas-sized flowers. Their deep blue, almost purple flowers tower above their foliage rather than snuggling within it. These bluebonnets grow along the lower slopes of the Chisos Mountains and desert hills, favoring alluvial soils found in washes and drainages. Sometimes they grow so thickly around runoff spots that it looks as if the mountains are crying purple tears. Desert marigolds bloom at this time, too, and favor the same areas, often dotting the purple-covered washes with flecks of gold. To add to the grandeur, yellow Fendler bladderpods erupt across the open lower-mountain slopes, turning brown foothills into a sea of pale yellow broken by the downsloping rivulets of bluish purple.

Big Bend bluebonnets peak around mid-March, often even earlier. Since Big Bend National Park lies far from Texas population centers, most Texans have to drive a long way to see them. Although I'm a native Texan and grew up with the requisite bluebonnet reverence, I didn't have the opportunity to see Big Bend bluebonnets until just recently. Even from a distance, their color was so intense I wondered if somebody had poured bluish purple paint into the mountain washes. When I hiked up to the blooms, their sweet, grapelike scent was intoxicating. I walked carefully among them, letting my hands gently brush the tops of their soft petals, thankful to have the opportunity to witness this spectacular display.

In April, the desert comes alive with wildflowers. At Dagger Flat in Big Bend National Park, thousands of yuccas congregate on the desert floor and dry mountain foothills, simultaneously displaying their huge, ivory-colored flower stalks. Around springs, seeps, and moist places within canyons, delicate columbines bloom. Unfortunately, this Texas treasure is declining due to unscrupulous collectors and high visitor traffic in Guadalupe and Big Bend National Parks.

About seventy-five species of cacti live in the region. Their thick, waxy skins and long, spiny leaves represent marvelous adaptations to little rainfall. Most bloom in spring, but tend to bloom more profusely with good rains. The ubiquitous prickly pear comes in several varieties and produces brilliant red, yellow, or yellow with red-centered flowers. Multijointed, uniquely shaped cholla cacti, some up to eight feet tall, burst forth with multiple clusters of magenta flowers from top to bottom. These odd, large cacti often stand alone, monuments to desert tenacity. Lower to the ground but no less attractive, claret-cup cacti produce scores of red blooms, while the Texas rainbow cactus yields delicate, pale yellow to orange flowers tinged with streaks of green.

Many people mistake the thorny ocotillo for a cactus, but it's really a superbly adapted woody shrub. During drought conditions, the spindly ocotillo loses its small, green leaves. In a severe, prolonged drought, even the stems turn brown and brittle, looking completely dead. But after a desert rain, the green

◁ *Big Bend bluebonnets* (Lupinus havardii) *and desert marigolds* (Baileya multiradiata), *Big Bend National Park.*

leaves reappear, and dense clusters of bright red flowers adorn the ends of the stems like brightly burning candle flames. With sufficient rains, ocotillos can bloom well into fall.

When rainfall soaks the ground, the creosote bush's bittersweet smell permeates the air, and the desert greens up almost immediately. Cenizo, also known as purple or Texas sage, spills forth with blooms following a rain. Most of the time, this nondescript bush with gray green leaves blends easily into the terrain. After a storm, however, purplish pink blooms explode all over it, turning the entire plant cotton-candy pink. The showy and well-named yellow rock nettle follows suit, adding splashes of gold to rocky crevices and cliffs all across the Big Bend area.

Some West Texas wildflowers not only need rain, but ample rain at the exact right time. In the Franklin Mountains, if fall and winter moisture is just right, large areas of Mexican gold poppies drape the slopes with glorious color in spring. Literally overnight, the Franklin foothills turn from brown to electric gold. This doesn't happen often, but when it does, it's a sight to behold. And even when the poppies do appear, the weather has to be perfect for viewing. Poppies close their petals at night and on cloudy days. Luckily for wildflower watchers, the sun usually shines in West Texas.

Other West Texas plants put their entire life energy into their flowers. Plants of the agave family, including its most prolific member, the lechuguilla, take many years to flower, but when they do, they produce spectacular results. The low-growing, utilitarian lechuguilla—its fibers long used for ropes and baskets—sends up a high stalk covered with a mass of purple or yellowish flowers at the top. It takes about twelve to fifteen years for the plant to store enough energy to create the massive bloom. Often the buds are so heavy that they bend the ten- to thirteen-foot-tall stalk, arcing it just enough to create a graceful downward curve.

Other agave species, sometimes known as century plants, take even longer to bloom, anywhere from twenty to forty years. Their tall, symmetrical flowers symbolize the West Texas desert. When conditions are just right, a four- to six-inch-thick stalk grows rapidly out of the spiny, rosette-shaped plant, reaching up to twenty feet high. Long, exquisitely arranged horizontal stems line the upper third of the stalk like a candelabra. Tightly packed clusters of tubular, upward-turning, yellow flowers grace the ends of the stems, accentuating the harmonious design. When the bloom wilts, the entire plant dies, exhausted from its reproductive zeal. Nobody can miss this flower. The agave's tall, solitary blossom, the culmination of its entire existence, enhances the West Texas horizon, drawing the eye just as surely as the surrounding mountain peaks.

❧❧❧

▷ Goat-foot morning glories (Ipomoea pes-caprae), *Matagorda Peninsula.*

Across Texas, wildflowers spring up on the desert floor, down mountainsides, along gurgling springs, on windswept prairies, and beneath verdant forest canopies. Most bloom for just a short while, then fade into obscurity, reminding us of life, death, and rebirth. Expansive distances and varied terrain ensure an incredible diversity of wildflowers in Texas, from much-celebrated bluebonnets to rare orchids. In every region, they grace the land with joyful color and exquisite form, inviting us to go out and explore our world.

◁ *Giant dagger yuccas* (Yucca faxoniana), *Dagger Flat, Big Bend National Park.*

△ *Bluebonnets* (Lupinus texensis), *Gillespie County, Hill Country.*

▷ ▷ *Datura or jimsonweed* (Datura wrightii), *Big Bend Ranch State Park.*

△ *Scarlet bouvardia* (Bouvardia ternifolia), *Davis Mountains.*

△ *Water lotus* (Nelumbo lutea), *Brazos Bend State Park.*

△ *Strawberry hedgehog cactus* (Echinocereus stramineus),
Big Bend National Park.

△ *Torrey yucca* (Yucca torreyi),
Bofecillos Mountains and Colorado Canyon, Big Bend Ranch State Park.

△ *Bluebonnets* (Lupinus texensis), *Indian paintbrush* (Castilleja indivisa),
and silver bladderpod (Lesquerella argyraea), *Llano County.*

▷ *Longspur columbine* (Aquilegia longissima), *Chisos Mountains, Big Bend National Park.*

▷ ▷ *Fendler bladderpod* (Lesquerella fendleri) *and Torrey yucca* (Yucca torreyi) *below Nugent Mountain, Big Bend National Park.*

◁ *Bluebonnets* (Lupinus subcarnosus), *Indian paintbrush* (Castilleja indivisa),
Drummond phlox (Phlox drummondii *var.* drummondii), *and*
buttercup (Ranunculus macranthus), *Gonzales County.*
△ *Basket flowers* (Centaurea americana) *below canyon wall, Palo Duro Canyon State Park.*

△ *Redbud tree* (Cercis canadensis), *Bear Creek, Hays County.*

▷ *Dogwood tree* (Cornus florida), *Wild Azalea Canyon, Newton County.*

◁ *Indian blanket* (Gaillardia pulchella) *and coreopsis*
(Coreopsis tinctoria) *with gourd plant, Travis County, Hill Country.*
△ *Goat-foot morning glories* (Ipomoea pes-caprae), *Boca Chica Beach near Brownsville.*
▷ ▷ *Prickly pear cactus* (Opuntia *sp.*), *Colorado Bend State Park.*

51

△ *Tansy aster* (Machaeranthera tanacetifolia) *and*
sand-bell (Nama hispidum), *Big Bend National Park.*
▷ *Native iris* (Iris hexagona), *Ottine Swamp, Palmetto State Park.*

◁ *Claret-cup cactus* (Echinocereus coccineus), *Big Bend National Park.*
△ *Bluebonnets* (Lupinus texensis), *Drummond phlox* (Phlox drummondii *var.* drummondii),
and spineless prickly pear (Opuntia *sp.*), *Travis County.*

△ *Sunflower* (Helianthus petiolaris), *Indian blanket* (Gaillardia pulchella), *and*
sleepy daisy (Xanthisma texanum), *Caprock Canyons State Park.*

△ *Scarlet bouvardia* (Bouvardia ternifolia), *Torrey yuccas*
(Yucca torreyi)*, and prickly pear cactus* (Opuntia *sp.*), *Davis Mountains.*
▷ ▷ *Feather dalea* (Dalea formosa), *Big Bend National Park.*

△ *The carnivorous floating bladderwort* (Utricularia radiata), *Black Cat Lake, Trinity County.*

△ *Water lilies* (Nymphaea odorata), *Black Cat Lake, Trinity County.*

△ *Bluebonnets* (Lupinus texensis), *Hays County.*
▷ *Bluebonnets* (Lupinus texensis) *and damianita* (Chrysactinia mexicana), *Travis County.*

◁ *Strawberry cactus* (Echinocereus stramineus), *Hot Springs, Big Bend National Park.*

△ *Mexican buckeye* (Ungnadia speciosa), *Chisos Mountains, Big Bend National Park.*

▷ ▷ *Longspur columbine* (Aquilegia longissima), *Chisos Mountains, Big Bend National Park.*

△ *Indian paintbrush* (Castilleja indivisa), *bluebonnets*
(Lupinus texensis), *and bladderpod* (Lesquerella argyraea), *Burnet County.*
▷ *Purple-tinged prickly pear* (Opuntia macrocentra *subspecies* violacea), *Big Bend National Park.*

◁ *Wild azaleas* (Rhododendron canescens) *with*
longleaf pine needles, Wild Azalea Canyon, Newton County.
△ *Fendler bladderpod* (Lesquerella fendleri), *sand-bell* (Nama hispidum),
and verbena (Glandularia bipinnatifida *var.* ciliata), *Big Bend National Park.*

73

△ *Margined perityle* (Perityle vaseyi), *Big Bend National Park.*

△ *Desert marigold* (Baileya multiradiata), *Big Bend National Park.*
▷ ▷ *Fendler bladderpod* (Lesquerella fendleri) *and Torrey yucca* (Yucca torreyi)
below Chisos Mountains, Big Bend National Park.

△ *Prairie spiderwort* (Tradescantia *sp.*), *Palmetto State Park.*

△ *Bluebonnets* (Lupinus texensis), *verbena* (Glandularia bipinnatifida *var.* bipinnatifida),
and bitterweed (Hymenoxys linearifolia), *Hays County, Hill Country.*

△ *Naked brittle-stem* (Psathyrotes scaposa) *and margined perityle* (Perityle vaseyi)
below Sierra Quemada, Big Bend National Park.

△ *Naked brittle-stem* (Psathyrotes scaposa), *Big Bend National Park.*

△ *Bluebonnets* (Lupinus texensis), *pink evening primroses* (Oenothera speciosa),
winecups (Callirhoe *sp.*), *and verbena*
(Glandularia bipinnatifida *var.* bipinnatifida), *Travis County.*

△ *Cenizo or sage* (Leucophyllum frutescens), *Santiago Mountains, Big Bend National Park.*
▷ ▷ *Margined perityle* (Perityle vaseyi) *near Castolon, Big Bend National Park.*

△ *Winecup* (Callirhoe involucrata), *yellow flax* (Linum hudsonioides), *and milk vetch*
(Astragalus nuttallianus), *Enchanted Rock State Natural Area.*
▷ *Foxglove* (Penstemon cobaea), *Travis County.*

◁ *Carnivorous pitcher plants* (Sarracenia alata), *Big Thicket National Preserve.*
△ *Claret-cup cactus* (Echinocereus coccineus) *below Cerro Diablo Peak, Cornudas Mountains.*

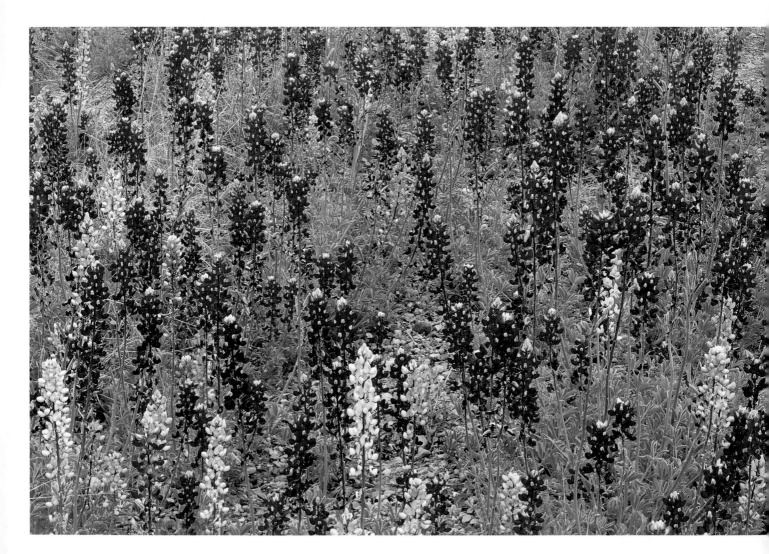

△ *Big Bend bluebonnets* (Lupinus havardii),
including albino variety, Big Bend National Park.
▷ *Mountain laurel or mescal bean* (Sophora secundiflora), *Hays County.*
▷ ▷ *Giant dagger yuccas* (Yucca faxoniana), *Dagger Flat, Big Bend National Park.*

◁ *Golden crownbeard* (Verbesina encelioides)
below Dead Horse Mountains, Big Bend National Park.
△ *Brown-eyed susans* (Rudbeckia hirta), *Hays County.*

△ *Horsemint* (Monarda citriodora), *Indian blanket* (Gaillardia pulchella), *and*
sleepy daisy (Xanthisma texanum), *Caprock Canyons State Park.*
▷ *Rainbow cactus* (Echinocereus dasyacanthus), *Big Bend National Park.*

◁ *Wild azaleas* (Rhododendron canescens), *Wild Azalea Canyon, Newton County.*
△ *Horsemint* (Monarda citriodora), *Travis County.*

△ *Western primrose* (Calylophus hartwegii), *Big Bend National Park.*
▷ *Giant dagger yuccas* (Yucca faxoniana), *Dagger Flat, Big Bend National Park.*

◁ *Indian paintbrush* (Castilleja indivisa), *Travis County.*
△ *Mountain laurel or mescal bean* (Sophora secundiflora) *with butterfly, Hays County.*
▷ ▷ *Sotol plants* (Dasylirion wheeleri) *and dayflower* (Commelina erecta),
Hueco Tanks State Historical Park.

△ *False dandelion* (Pyrrhopappus pauciflorus), *Hays County.*

△ *Stream orchis orchid* (Epipactis gigantea), *Big Bend National Park.*

△ *Cut-leaved daisy* (Engelmannia peristenia), *Travis County.*

△ *Dogwood tree* (Cornus florida), *Newton County.*

△ *Phlox* (Phlox roemeriana), *Hays County.*

▷ *Bluebonnets* (Lupinus texensis) *and white prickly poppies* (Argemone albiflora), *Gillespie County, Hill Country.*

▷ ▷ *Bluebonnets* (Lupinus texensis) *and yuccas* (Yucca treculeana)
along a county road, Gillespie County.